THE HEAD IN THE SAND

A Roman play

Julia Donaldson

For Arthur Godbold's daughter Mary – J.D.

ABOUT THE AUTHOR

Julia Donaldson is the author of the award-winning picture book *The Gruffalo*, as well as many other books for children. She is a prolific songwriter, especially for BBC Children's TV programmes, and she has written many plays for a variety of educational publishers for use in schools.

THE HEAD IN THE SAND

A Roman play

Julia Donaldson

Illustrated by Ross Collins

HODDER
Wayland

an imprint of Hodder Children's Books

Editor: Gill Munton
Designer: Don Martin

Published in Great Britain in 2003
by Hodder Wayland, an imprint of
Hodder Children's Books

A catalogue record for this book is available
from the British Library.

ISBN: 0 7502 4126 8 (hb)

Printed and bound in Hong Kong by Shek Wah Tong

Hodder Children's Books
A division of Hodder Headline Limited
338 Euston Road, London NW1 3BH

INTRODUCTION

In 1907, a boy called Arthur Godbold discovered a bronze head in the sand at the edge of the River Alde. Today it can be seen in the British Museum, where it is described as the "head of the Emperor Claudius". How did Claudius's head end up in a Suffolk river? And what happened to the real Claudius?

In this play, Arthur and his friend Gertie discover the answers to these questions as the first 17 years of the Roman occupation of Britain, including Boudicca's rebellion, are played out before their eyes. The play also follows Arthur's own story and shows what happened to the head after he excavated it.

Arthur Godbold was a real person, and so was Gertie (whose full name was Violet Gertrude Osborn). They may not have actually met until several years later when he had a milk round and she was a maid at the local vicarage. They married in 1919. Arthur really did whitewash the head and sell it for five shillings, and it really did fetch £15,500 at a Sotheby's auction in 1965 (a record price at the time).

The play is set in the kitchen of the Godbold family in the village of Rendham, Suffolk, in 1907. Action simultaneously takes place in Roman Britain, and at various points in the play the kitchen is transformed into other locations (e.g. a river bank, a modern-day auction house, a Roman forum). This can be indicated through minimal changes of scenery and the judicious use of props and mime. See pages 16 and 47 for suggestions.

The play is written to run seamlessly, but it has been divided into three scenes for convenience when children are reading it.

There are 33 speaking parts. Because society in Roman Britain was male-dominated, there are more male than female roles, but the balance can be redressed if some of the soldiers' and the tribal leaders' parts are acted by girls.

The play can, however, be read in small groups, with some children taking more than one role.

THE CAST

Name	Description	Role
Twentieth-century characters		
Arthur Godbold	A boy	Large
Gertie Osborn	A girl	Large
Mrs. Holland	A rich woman	Medium
Auctioneer	(Female)	Small
Romans		
Claudius	A Roman Emperor	Large
Valeria Messalina	Claudius's third wife	Medium
Agrippina	Claudius's fourth wife	Small
Nero	A Roman Emperor and Agrippina's son	Medium

Aulus Plautius	Commanding Officer and first Governor of Britain	Medium
Recruiting Officer	(Male or female)	Medium
Lucius	A soldier in the Twentieth Valeria legion	Large
Didius	⎫	Medium
Tadius		Medium
Ursus	Soldiers	Medium
Marcus	(Male or female)	Medium
Mannius		Medium
Varius		Medium
Cornelius	⎭	Medium
A messenger	(Male or female)	Medium
Pomponius	A retired army officer	Medium
Julia	His wife	Medium
Octavius	⎫ Friends of Pomponius	Medium
Flavia	⎭ and Julia	Medium

Ancient Britons

Atrebates leader	⎫	Small
Cantiaci leader		Small
Trinovantes leader	(Male or female)*	Small
Iceni leader		Small
Catuvellauni leader	⎭	Small
Boudicca	Queen of the Iceni	Large
Prasutagus	King of the Iceni	Medium
Huctia (aged 7)	⎫ Daughters of Boudicca	Medium
Vilbia (aged 9)	⎭ and Prasutagus	Medium
Jamcilla (from the Trinovantes)	The slave of Julia and Pomponius	Medium

*Followers of the five tribes may be played by members of the cast.

SCENE 1 *Invasion*

(**Arthur, Gertie, Valeria, Claudius, Aulus, a Recruiting Officer, Lucius, Didius, Tadius, Marcus, Ursus, Mannius, Varius, Cornelius, Leader of the Catuvellauni, Leader of the Trinovantes, Leader of the Iceni, Leader of the Atrebates, Leader of the Cantiaci)**

*The year is 1907. The Godbolds' kitchen. Enter **Arthur**, staggering under the weight of an object wrapped in a cloth. There is a knock at the door. **Arthur** puts the object on the table and goes to open the door. Enter **Gertie**.*

Arthur: Hello, Gertie.

Gertie: Hello, Arthur. Do you want to come and play by the river?

Arthur: I've just *been* playing by the river. You'll never guess what I found there.

Gertie: A swan's nest?

Arthur: No.

Gertie: An old boot?

Arthur: No – a head.

Gertie: A head! A human head?

SCENE 1

Arthur: Yes. Well, sort of. I dug it out of the sand with a hoe.

Gertie: A skull! Maybe someone's been murdered! Let's tell the police!

Arthur: Don't you want to see it first?

Gertie: Yes! I don't know … I'm not too keen on skulls. All right, then.

Arthur: Here it is.

(**Arthur** *removes the cloth, revealing a bronze head.*)

Gertie: *(Disappointed)* That's not a skull.

Arthur: I never said it was!

Gertie: It's made of metal.

Arthur: Yes – bronze, I'd say. It's a man, isn't it?

Gertie: He's got nice thick hair.

Arthur: But no proper eyes – just holes.

Gertie: His neck's all broken and jagged.

Arthur: Look at his funny sticking-out ears!

The Roman year is now AD 43.

Valeria: *(Offstage)* Have you lost your head, Claudius?

Gertie: Who's that?

Arthur: I don't know!

(**Valeria** *sweeps in.*)

Valeria: Claudius! Claudius! Where is he? And who are you two? No, don't tell me – I can guess. Claudius has taken on a couple of extra slaves without telling me. That's typical.

Arthur: Excuse me – who are you?

Valeria: Hasn't he even told you about me? I'm Valeria, the Emperor's wife. Ah, here he is.

*(Enter **Claudius**. **Arthur** and **Gertie** stare, dumbstruck.)*

Valeria: Claudius, have you completely lost your head?

Claudius: No, my darling little V-V-Valeria, it still seems to be sitting on my shoulders.

Valeria: Then why are you planning to invade Britain?

Claudius: Well, it's just about the only place left. We've got G-G-Greece, and Spain, and France, and Germany, and great ch-ch-chunks of Africa, and …

Valeria: Yes, yes, I know. Isn't that enough for you?

Claudius: No, it's not. Those places don't really c-c-count. They were all conquered before I became Emperor. I didn't get any of the g-g-glory. I want to have a victory parade! A proper big one, with elephants! I want to be Claudius the C-C-Conqueror, Claudius the Great, Claudius the God, instead of just C-C-C-C ...

Valeria: Claudius with the sticking-out ears. I know.

Claudius: I wasn't going to s-s-say that.

Arthur: *(Whispering to **Gertie**)* It's him, isn't it?

Gertie: Who?

Arthur: *(Still whispering, pointing to the head and then to **Claudius**)* My head – it's him! It's that Roman Emperor! It's his head!

Valeria: I wish there was more *between* your sticking-out ears, Claudius. Listen. We've already been to Britain. We've done that.

Claudius: Have we? I don't remember.

Valeria: Not you, personally; I'm talking about your ancestor Julius Caesar. He didn't think it was worth staying there. So what makes you think you know so much better? Just think of all the soldiers you'll need! Where are they going to come from?

Claudius: Good point, my dear – you're not just a p-p-pretty little head. I'll ask my Commanding Officer. Aulus! Aulus!

*(Enter **Aulus Plautius**.)*

11

Aulus: Yes, Your Imperial Highness.

Claudius: How many legions would we need to invade Britain?

Aulus: I should say four regular legions, Your Highness, plus the same number of auxiliaries.

Valeria: You see? I said you were mad. That's nearly 50,000 men. Where are you going to find them all?

Claudius: Wh-wh-what do you think, Aulus?

Aulus: Well, we'd need to do a bit of juggling around. I'm pretty sure we could spare some legions from here and there. The Twentieth Valeria, for instance. We could move them from Germany.

Claudius: You see, my d-d-dear – the Twentieth Valeria! The same name as yours! That must be a good omen!

Aulus: We may need to recruit some extra men, of course.

Claudius: You d-d-do that. Oh, and see if you can organise a few elephants for the victory parade. Now, come along, Valeria, or we'll miss the g-g-gladiator show.

Valeria: I still say you've lost your head.

*(Exit **Claudius**, **Valeria** and **Aulus**. Enter the **Recruiting Officer**, carrying the Eagle of the Twentieth Valeria.)*

Recruiting Officer: *(To Arthur)* Name?

Arthur: Who, me? I'm Arthur Godbold.

SCENE 1

Recruiting Officer: What sort of a name is that? Are you sure you're a Roman citizen?

Arthur: No, I'm not.

Gertie: He doesn't want to join the army, anyway.

Recruiting Officer: Well, be off and stop wasting my time, then.

*(**Arthur** and **Gertie** withdraw.)*

Recruiting Officer: Next, please!

*(Enter **Lucius**.)*

Recruiting Officer: Name?

Lucius: Lucius Vitalis.

Recruiting Officer: Age?

Lucius: I'm 18.

Recruiting Officer: So, Lucius, what makes you want to join the Twentieth Valeria? You know it's one of the legions that's going to invade Britain, don't you?

Lucius: Yes – I fancy a bit of travel.

Recruiting Officer: You might end up travelling into the next world.

Lucius: I'm not scared of battle.

Recruiting Officer: Well, let's have a look at you. Hmmm, bright eyes – that's good. You're nice and tall, too. Your chest's on the weedy side, but it'll do, I suppose. Yes, you look like a reasonable specimen. Will you be up to marching 30 kilometres a day?

Lucius: I think I can manage that.

SCENE 1

Recruiting Officer: Your armour will be quite heavy, you realise. And you'll be carrying your sword and shield, plus a couple of javelins. Not forgetting your bedroll, and food for three days. Oh, and a bucket, and a few tools and a pickaxe.

Lucius: Anything else?

Recruiting Officer: Yes. Tent pegs. You're going to be camping, not staying in hotels, you know.

Lucius: What will I be paid?

Recruiting Officer: 100 denarii a year.

Lucius: That's not bad!

Recruiting Officer: You'll have to pay for your uniform and weapons out of that, of course.

Lucius: Of course.

Recruiting Officer: And your food.

Lucius: Oh.

Recruiting Officer: And then there's a charge for your share of a tent. Oh, and your contribution to the burial fund.

Lucius: How much will I have left from the hundred denarii after all that?

Recruiting Officer: About 25. Do you still want to join?

Lucius: Er … yes.

Recruiting Officer: Then repeat after me: I swear to be loyal to the Emperor, to my comrades and to the Eagle of the Twentieth Valeria.

Lucius: I swear to be loyal to the Emperor, to my comrades and to the Eagle of the Twentieth Valeria.

SCENE 1

Recruiting Officer: You're in!

> *(Exit the **Recruiting Officer**. **Lucius** starts to march on the spot. He is joined by **Didius**, **Tadius**, **Marcus**, **Ursus**, **Mannius**, **Varius** and **Cornelius**, who all keep in step with him.)*

Soldiers: *(Chanting in time to their marching)*
> Eight men in a tent,
> Ten tents in a century,
> Six centuries in a cohort,
> Ten cohorts in a legion!
> Our legion is superior –
> Up with the Twentieth Valeria!

Lucius: What's this Britain place like, anyway?

Didius: I've heard there are no proper roads.

Tadius: Or towns.

Marcus: Or baths.

Ursus: My mum says it's cold and wet – she's packed me some woolly underpants.

Mannius: I've heard the Britons are really fierce.

Varius: They've got wild, spiky hair.

Cornelius: And amazing blue war paint.

Ursus: I wish I'd stayed at home with Mum.

Didius: They come rushing at you, driving their chariots and whirling their swords and screaming battle cries. Women and all.

Lucius: *(In disbelief)* They have women in the army?

Tadius: If you can call it an army. It's just a lot of tribes, really – that's what I've heard.

Lucius: Tribes? What tribes?

*(The **soldiers** march off.)*

*(**The Atrebates, the Cantiaci, the Trinovantes** and **the Iceni** race on, whirling swords and threatening each other.)*

The Atrebates: At-At-At-re-ba-tes!

The Cantiaci: Can-Can-Can-ti-a-ci!

The Trinovantes: Tri-Tri-Tri-no-van-tes!

The Iceni: I-I-I-ce-ni!

*(Enter **the Catuvellauni**.)*

The Catuvellauni: Catuvellauni are the best.
Up with the Cats and down with the rest!

*(**The Atrebates, the Cantiaci, the Trinovantes** and **the Iceni** cower. **Arthur** and **Gertie** creep*

*forwards, and the **Leader of the Catuvellauni** points at them.)*

Leader of the Catuvellauni: What tribe are they in?

Leader of the Trinovantes: Maybe they're a pair of wandering Druids.

Arthur: Excuse me – why are you all fighting each other when you're about to be attacked by the Romans?

Leader of the Iceni: I'm not too bothered about the Romans. Between you and me, I'm planning to do a deal with them, so they'll let us Iceni hang on to our kingdom.

Leader of the Atrebates: I'm not too bothered about the Romans. Between you and me, it was my tribe who invited them. We're sick of being bossed about by this lot here. *(Indicating **the Catuvellauni)***

Leader of the Catuvellauni: I'm not too bothered about the Romans. Between you and me, I've heard that they can't round up enough troops.

Soldiers: *(Offstage)* That's what they think.

*(Exit the five **tribes**, chanting their chants. **Arthur** and **Gertie** withdraw.)*

*(Enter **Lucius, Didius, Tadius, Ursus, Marcus, Mannius, Varius** and **Cornelius**, who start to bang in tent pegs.)*

Lucius: Well, that could have been worse. We got across the Channel all right.

Didius: We got London all right.

Tadius: Yes, and now we're going to get ...

Ursus: Blisters! It's terrible, isn't it? Blisters on your feet from marching and blisters on your hands from banging in tent pegs.

Tadius: I didn't mean that. I meant we were going to get Colchester. That's the plan, isn't it?

Marcus: Yes, but we've got to wait till the Emperor arrives with the elephants.

Lucius: The elephants?

Mannius: That's right. He wants to ride one of them in triumph into Colchester.

*(Enter **Aulus** and **Claudius**. The **soldiers** stand to attention.)* `

Aulus: Attention, valiant soldiers all! His Imperial Highness has arrived.

Claudius: Well done, everyone. So far, so good. And now it's time to feed the ch-ch-chickens. Come and be fed, my pretties.

*(**Claudius** throws down food for his chickens.)*

Lucius: Why is he doing that?

Varius: To see if we're going to win the battle. If the chickens gobble up all the food, it's a sign of victory. If they leave any, it means we'll be defeated.

Claudius: Look at that! Peck, peck, peck! Gobble, gobble, gobble! Have you ever seen such appetites? You'd think they'd been starved for weeks!

Cornelius: *(Under his breath)* They probably have.

Claudius: The chickens are telling us that the gods are on our side. We're going to give them the beating of their lives!

Didius: Who? The chickens?

Claudius: No – the British warriors. And what are we going to do when we reach Colchester?

Tadius: Kill everyone?

Claudius: No.

Marcus: Burn the place down?

Claudius: No, no, no! Do birds destroy their own nests? Remember, you're going to be staying in Britain once we've c-c-conquered it. No – you tell them, Aulus.

Aulus: We're going to civilise them! We're going to build roads! We're going to build temples! We're going to build law courts!

Mannius: What about a few drains?

Aulus: Yes, drains, too.

Varius: Underfloor heating?

Aulus: That sort of thing.

Ursus: How about introducing a few of those scraper things – you know, for scraping the dirt off you in the bath? My mum said they haven't got any of those.

Aulus: And she was quite right. Civilisation, that's the name of the game. So remember, the Emperor wants prisoners, not corpses. You can't civilise corpses. I think they've got the general idea, Your Imperial Highness.

Claudius: Very good. In that case, onwards to C-C-Colchester!

Soldiers: Onwards to C-C-Colchester!

*(The **soldiers** march off. Exit **Claudius** and **Aulus**.)*

*(Enter the **Leaders of the Atrebates, the Cantiaci, the Trinovantes, the Iceni** and **the Catuvellauni**. They have been conquered and they look and sound dejected – except for the **Leader of the Iceni**.)*

Leader of the Atrebates: At-At-At-re-ba-tes!

Leader of the Cantiaci: Can-Can-Can-ti-a-ci!

Leader of the Trinovantes: Tri-Tri-Tri-no-van-tes!

Leader of the Iceni: I-I-I-ce-ni!

Leader of the Catuvellauni: Catuvellauni were the best. How did we lose like all the rest?

*(Enter **Claudius** and **Aulus**.)*

Claudius: Welcome to C-C-Colchester.

*(The **Leaders of the Trinovantes, the Cantiaci, the Atrebates** and **the Catuvellauni** go down on one knee.)*

Leader of the Trinovantes:
Leader of the Cantiaci:
Leader of the Atrebates:
Leader of the Catuvellauni:
} *(Unenthusiastically)* Hail, mighty Claudius.

Claudius: Do you surrender your kingdoms to be governed by Aulus here, as part of the Roman Empire?

Leader of the Trinovantes:
Leader of the Cantiaci:
Leader of the Atrebates:
Leader of the Catuvellauni: } We do.

Leader of the Trinovantes: Hey, what about him?

Leader of the Cantiaci: Who?

Leader of the Trinovantes: The Iceni chief.

Leader of the Atrebates: Yes – go on, you – down on your knees.

Leader of the Catuvellauni: You're no different from us. Your kingdom's been swallowed up by Rome, too.

Leader of the Iceni: I think you'll find you're mistaken.

Aulus: Yes. Let me explain. In recognition of their assistance in our campaign, the Iceni are to be allowed to hang on to their kingdom.

Leader of the Trinovantes:
Leader of the Cantiaci:
Leader of the Atrebates:
Leader of the Catuvellauni: } That's not fair!

Claudius: So that's settled, then. I'll leave you all in the c-c-capable hands of Aulus. It's time the elephants and I got back for our victory parade.

Aulus: Er … Your Highness, you've just had a victory parade.

Claudius: Ah, you're talking about the Colchester victory parade. I'm going to have another one – in Rome.

*(Exit **the tribe Leaders, Aulus** and **Claudius**.)*

SCENE 2 *Unrest*

(Vilbia, Huctia, Boudicca, Tadius, Marcus, Didius, Mannius, Ursus, Varius, Lucius, Cornelius, Arthur, Gertie, Julia, Jamcilla, a messenger, Prasutagus, Mrs. Holland, Claudius, Valeria, Agrippina, Nero)

*The Roman year is AD 48. **Prasutagus** is now Leader of the Iceni. Enter **Boudicca** with **Vilbia** and **Huctia**. **Boudicca** is carrying a shield. They are on the banks of a river. **Arthur** and **Gertie** are still on stage, in the background.*

Vilbia: That's Father's shield, isn't it?

Huctia: Yes, it's his beautiful shield with the raven on it. I love that shield.

Boudicca: Hush, stop chattering, children. You're disturbing the peace of the river goddess.

Vilbia: Are we going to put the shield in the river, Mother?

Boudicca: Yes, we're offering it to the goddess.

Vilbia: I don't want the goddess to have the shield. I want Father to keep it.

23

Huctia: Yes – maybe he'll need it to fight the Romans.

Boudicca: We Iceni are at peace with the Romans.

Huctia: Will we always be at peace with them?

Boudicca: As long as they allow us to remain free.

Vilbia: Where is Father?

Boudicca: He's lying down. He's had the pain in his heart again.

Huctia: Is that why we're giving the shield to the river goddess?

Boudicca: Yes. Now, throw your corn seeds into the river, Huctia, and pour in the wine, Vilbia, while I place the shield in the water.

*(**Boudicca** puts the shield in the river.)*

Boudicca: Goddess of the river, take our corn.
    Goddess of water, take our wine.
    Goddess of life, take my husband's shield.
    May his heart grow strong as the oak trees
    on your banks.
    May the Iceni people stay free as the birds
    in your reeds.

Vilbia: Is that the end?

Boudicca: Not quite. We must all drink from the water.

> *(**Boudicca**, **Vilbia** and **Huctia** scoop up water with their hands and drink.)*

Huctia: Let's run home now and see if Father's better.

> *(**Vilbia** and **Huctia** run off. **Boudicca** walks slowly after them.)*

> *The Roman year is now AD 49. Enter **Tadius**, **Marcus**, **Didius**, **Mannius**, **Ursus**, **Varius**, **Lucius** and **Cornelius**, marching towards their barracks in Colchester.*

Tadius: I can't see the point of these marches.

Marcus: It's to keep us fit for battle.

Didius: But we never have any battles. We're stuck in
    Colchester all the time. We've been there for
    six years.

Mannius: We'll probably be there till we retire.

Ursus: I still miss my mum.

Varius: Don't grumble. It's not such a bad place.
    Not now it's been rebuilt. It's almost like a
    Roman town now.

Lucius: I wouldn't mind settling down there myself when I retire.

Cornelius: That couldn't have anything to do with a certain slave girl, could it?

Lucius: *(Blushing)* What do you mean?

Cornelius: The one I've seen you chatting to at the oyster stall.

Lucius: I don't know what you're on about.

Cornelius: Aha, so I'm right!

Didius: Here we are, back at the barracks.

*(The **soldiers** stop marching and sit down to take their boots off.)*

Tadius: Look, the duty roster is up.

*(The **soldiers** go to look at the roster.)*

Marcus: I'm on guard duty.

Mannius: I'm collecting wood.

Ursus: Oh, no! I'm cleaning out the lavs again!

Varius: Hey, Cornelius, you and I are down to join that canal-digging team. And Lucius, you're going to be at the new temple.

Lucius: Doing what?

Varius: Installing a statue, it says.

Lucius: Let's have a look. Oh, yes. "Bronze statue of Claudius on horseback to be transported from Gaius Aurelius's workshop and installed in the temple." Right, I'd best be off!

*(Exit **Lucius**.)*

Marcus: He's in a hurry!

Cornelius: And I can guess why. You know where that workshop is?

Marcus: No.

Cornelius: Next door to the oyster stall!

*(Exit the **soldiers** to their various duties.)*

*(**Arthur** and **Gertie** move back centre-stage, and **Arthur** holds out the bronze head.)*

Arthur: Did you hear that? A bronze statue!

Gertie: A statue of Claudius!

Arthur: So that's where this head comes from!

Gertie: It's funny to think that it was brand new once.

Arthur: It looks a bit tatty now, doesn't it?

Gertie: Why don't we paint it?

Arthur: Good idea. There's a pot of whitewash here.

*(**Arthur** and **Gertie** start to paint the head, laughing.)*

27

Arthur: Here's some hair dye for you, Claudius.

Gertie: And foundation cream.

Arthur: Lipstick ...

Gertie: We can't give him any eye make-up because he hasn't got any eyes.

*The forum in Colchester. Enter **Julia** and **Jamcilla**.*

*(**Arthur** and **Gertie** withdraw.)*

Julia: Is my eye make-up all right, Jamcilla?

Jamcilla: Yes, madam. But it's your ladies' bath morning, isn't it? Won't your make-up all wash off in the baths?

Julia: I'm just going for the gossip; I shan't be taking a dip. Now, meet me back here when you've done the shopping.

Jamcilla: Yes, madam.

*(Exit **Julia**. Enter **Lucius**.)*

Lucius: Hello, Jamcilla.

Jamcilla: Lucius! What are you doing here?

Lucius: I've been putting up a bronze statue of Claudius in the new temple.

Jamcilla: Oh, that.

Lucius: You don't sound too enthusiastic about the mighty man.

Jamcilla: I'm not. I was a free woman before you Romans came and took the place over. My father was killed in the fighting, and my mother couldn't afford to bring us all up. That's why I was sold to be a slave.

28

SCENE 2

Lucius: Jamcilla, I don't want you to be a slave for the rest of your life. I want us to get married.

Jamcilla: That's all very well, Lucius, but you know you're not allowed to marry when you're in the army. We'd need to wait nearly twenty years.

Lucius: I know, but maybe I could pay to have you freed before then. We could start a family and get married later.

Jamcilla: I've heard that one before! What if you get sent to the other side of the country?

Lucius: I won't. The Twentieth Valeria is staying in Colchester. I'm serious, Jamcilla. I want us to be together.

*(Enter **Cornelius** and **Varius**.)*

Cornelius: I thought we might find you here, Lucius! Phew, that canal digging is back-breaking.

Varius: Well, what do you think about the news?

Lucius: What news?

Varius: The Twentieth is off to the west!

Cornelius: There's been some trouble with the tribes over there and they're moving us. Well, don't just stand there like a statue! Aren't you going to introduce us to your ladyfriend?

Jamcilla: *(Bitterly)* There's no time for that. I've got shopping to do. Goodbye, Lucius.

*(Exit **Jamcilla** one way, the **soldiers** the other.)*

*In the land of the Iceni. Enter a **messenger**.*

Messenger: News! News for the Iceni!

29

SCENE 2

*(Enter **Prasutagus**, **Boudicca**, **Vilbia** and **Huctia**.)*

Messenger: News from the new Governor of Britain. Where is the King of the Iceni?

Prasutagus: I am the King.

Boudicca: And I am Boudicca, his wife. What is your news?

Messenger: Your tribe is to hand over all its weapons.

Boudicca: Hand them over? To whom?

Messenger: To the Romans.

Boudicca: Why? We are not at war with the Romans. Our weapons are to protect us from the other tribes.

Prasutagus: What do the Romans have to fear from us? There are a thousand Roman soldiers not far away, in Colchester. They are well trained, and armed. We would be foolish to attack them, even if we wanted to.

Messenger: But the thing is, those thousand men are going to be moved. There's been trouble with the tribes in the west.

Prasutagus: Ah, so the Romans fear we will attack Colchester while they are away.

Boudicca: They don't trust us! That's it, isn't it?

Messenger: You may think what you like.

Boudicca: *(Bitterly)* As long as we do what we're told – I know. You may go now.

*(Exit the **messenger**.)*

Huctia: We won't hand over our weapons, will we, Father?

Prasutagus: We have no choice.

Vilbia: Can we make some more in secret?

Boudicca: She's got a clever head on her shoulders, that daughter of ours.

Prasutagus: She takes after you!

(*Exit **Prasutagus**, **Boudicca**, **Vilbia** and **Huctia**.*)

*The Godbolds' kitchen. **Arthur** and **Gertie** are admiring the newly painted head. There is a knock at the back door.*

Arthur: There's someone knocking at the door. That's funny – the others just came gliding through it.

Gertie: Better have a peep before you open it.

(***Arthur** looks through the keyhole.*)

Gertie: Well, is it an Ancient Roman or an Ancient Briton?

Arthur: Neither. It's ancient Mrs. Holland from the big house. (*He opens the door*)

Mrs. Holland: Hello, my dears. I've heard about your find. Can I have a look?

Arthur: Yes – here it is. (*He shows her the head*)

Mrs. Holland: Good heavens – what have you done? You've covered it in paint, you silly children. We'll have to get that off for a start.

Arthur: I like it like that.

Gertie: It's Arthur's head, Mrs. Holland. He found it, so he can do what he likes with it.

Mrs. Holland: Don't be cheeky, Gertie. You'll have to start minding your manners if you want to get a maid's job when you leave school.

*(**Gertie** looks sulky.)*

Mrs. Holland: How would you like to sell the head, Arthur?

Arthur: Sell it? How much for?

Mrs. Holland: Shall we say four shillings?

Arthur: Four bob! That's nearly a year's pocket money!

Gertie: No! Don't let her have it, Arthur.

Mrs. Holland: Now, then, Gertie – as you pointed out, it's Arthur's head and he can do what he likes with it. Well, Arthur?

Arthur: I don't know … I'll have to think about it, Mrs. Holland.

Mrs. Holland: What if we made it five shillings?

Arthur: Yes – you're on!

Mrs. Holland: Here you are – two shiny half-crowns.

Arthur: Thanks, Mrs. Holland. *(He gives her the head)*

Mrs. Holland: Thank you, Arthur. Goodbye, Gertie – and watch that tongue of yours!

*(Exit **Mrs. Holland**, carrying the head.)*

Gertie: I've had enough of you, Arthur Godbold. *(Starting to walk away)*

Arthur: Hey, don't go! What's the matter?

Gertie: How could you? How could you let that woman make away with Claudius? I'm never going to speak to you again!

*(Exit **Gertie**. **Arthur** looks dejected.)*

*The Roman year is now AD 60. Enter **Claudius**. Although he has been dead for six years, he appears unchanged.*

Claudius: How c-c-could I? How could I let a woman make away with me?

Arthur: Make away with you? What – kill you, do you mean?

Claudius: That's right. I ate a dish of poisoned mushrooms, prepared by my own w-w-wife.

Arthur: Who, Valeria?

*(Enter **Valeria**.)*

Valeria: No, not me. In fact, if you care to remember, Claudius, it was *you* who had *me* killed.

Claudius: You asked for it. Carrying on with all those other men, and p-p-plotting against me.

SCENE 2

Valeria: Well, you didn't do much better with your next wife, did you?

*(Enter **Agrippina** and **Nero**.)*

Agrippina: That's me, Agrippina. And this is my son Nero. He was 11 when I married Claudius.

Nero: *(To **Agrippina**)* And I was 16 when you bumped him off.

Agrippina: I did it for you, my pet — so that you could become Emperor.

Nero: After which, I bumped *you* off. Now, hop it, you three — you're all dead; you shouldn't be hanging around. I'm singing at the theatre this afternoon; I need to practise.

*(Exit **Agrippina**, **Valeria** and **Claudius**.)*

Nero: *(To **Arthur**)* Listen to this, slave.

"Rome is burning, Rome is burning,
Fetch the engines, fetch the engines.
Fire, fire! Fire, fire!
Pour on water, pour on water."

Don't you think I'm in fine voice?

*(**Arthur** is saved from answering by the entrance of the **messenger**. **Arthur** withdraws.)*

Messenger: Your Highness! Your Highness! News from Britain! The King of the Iceni has died.

Nero: Jolly good. Did he make a will?

Messenger: Yes, Your Highness. He's left you half of his money, goods and land.

Nero: Only half? Who gets the other half?

Messenger: His two daughters.

Nero: Doesn't he have any sons?

Messenger: No, Your Highness.

Nero: Then who's going to be the next King of the Iceni?

Messenger: His widow, Boudicca, has declared herself Queen.

Nero: What nonsense! Go and tell Boudicca that from now on her tribe is part of the Roman Empire.

Messenger: What if she doesn't agree?

Nero: Then the Governor can have her flogged. He can have those daughters of hers roughed up, too. That should put her in her place. Now, if you've quite finished wasting my time, perhaps I can get to the theatre. It's going to be packed, and I've given orders that no one can leave until I've finished singing.

"Rome is burning, Rome is burning,
Fetch the engines, fetch the engines ..."

*(Exit **Nero**, singing. Exit the **messenger**.)*

SCENE 3 *Rebellion*

(**Arthur, Gertie, Pomponius, Jamcilla, Julia, Flavia, Octavius, Leader of the Trinovantes, Boudicca, Vilbia, Huctia, Ursus, Tadius, Marcus, Mannius, Varius, Didius, Lucius, Cornelius, an auctioneer, Claudius**)

The Godbolds' kitchen. ***Arthur*** *is still on stage. There is a knock at the door and* ***Arthur*** *opens it. Enter* ***Gertie***.

Arthur: Oh, it's you. Are you talking to me again?

Gertie: I suppose so. Did you know they've been dredging the river? They're looking for more Roman remains. And guess what they've found!

Arthur: Claudius's body?

Gertie: No.

Arthur: Boudicca's shield?

Gertie: No – oyster shells! Masses and masses of oyster shells!

(***Arthur*** *and* ***Gertie*** *withdraw.*)

(*Enter* ***Julia*** *and* ***Pomponius*** *and their guests* ***Flavia*** *and* ***Octavius***. *They recline in readiness for a meal. Enter* ***Jamcilla***.)

Pomponius: More oysters, Jamcilla! No, more than that! Heap them on.

Jamcilla: *(Serving him)* Is that enough, sir?

Pomponius: It's enough to be getting on with. Pity there's not more wine in the sauce. Remind me to speak to the cook about that, Julia.

Julia: It tastes fine to me. Would you like some more oysters, Flavia?

Flavia: No, thank you. What a beautiful water jug!

Julia: Yes, isn't it? It's from Gaius Aurelius's workshop in the forum. He's such a wonderful craftsman! He made the statue of Claudius for the temple.

Octavius: Talking of the temple, have you heard all this talk about the Trinovantes tribe?

Julia: The Trinovantes – weren't they your people, Jamcilla, before we bought you?

Jamcilla: Yes, madam.

Pomponius: So what's this talk you've been listening to, Octavius?

Octavius: Well, I've heard there may be some sort of rebellion brewing. It seems they're angry about their chiefs having to serve as priests in the temple.

Pomponius: Oh, that old story. It won't come to anything. I heard that the Iceni were on the warpath, but that hasn't happened, either. This sauce is awfully sticky.

*(**Pomponius** wipes his hands on **Jamcilla's** hair. **Jamcilla** shudders.)*

Pomponius: Now, enough of this doom and gloom. Fill up the glasses, Jamcilla, and bring on the beef – and plenty of fish sauce to go with it.

Julia: Go easy on the fish sauce, Pomponius, or you'll get your liver trouble again. You know how you hate that mustard mouthwash.

(A distant chanting is heard.)

Trinovantes leader and followers: *(Offstage)* Tri-Tri-Tri-no-van-tes!

Boudicca and Iceni followers: *(Offstage)* I-I-I-ce-ni!

Flavia: What was that?

Pomponius: Just some hooligans. The night watchman will deal with them.

All Trinovantes: *(Offstage, more loudly)* Tri-Tri-Tri-no-van-tes …

All Iceni: *(Offstage, more loudly)* I-I-I-ce-ni …

Flavia: It sounds like an awful lot of them.

Julia: *(Going to the window and looking out)* By Jupiter! There are thousands of them!

*(**Pomponius**, **Octavius** and **Flavia** join her.)*

Flavia: Look at those chariots!

Octavius: And those torches! They're setting fire to the buildings!

Pomponius: Everyone's running away from them! It's crazy out there!

Julia: That old man's not running away. He's standing up to them!

Pomponius: Yes, and they've made short work of him. And look, there go a couple of children under the chariot wheels!

Flavia: They're coming this way! Quick, let's get out of here!

Julia: But where shall we go?

Octavius: Let's just follow the others. Where are they heading?

Flavia: The temple! Let's go!

*(**Pomponius**, **Octavius** and **Flavia** run off.)*

Julia: Are you coming, Jamcilla?

Jamcilla: Yes, madam.

*(**Julia** follows the others, leaving **Jamcilla** on her own.)*

Jamcilla: But not with you. I'm going to join my own people!

*(**Jamcilla** runs out. The battle cries are deafening.)*

*The outskirts of Colchester. Enter **Boudicca**, **Vilbia** and **Huctia** (now young women) and **Iceni followers** with the **Trinovantes leader** and **followers**. **Boudicca** carries the bronze head of Claudius on a pike.*

The Trinovantes: Tri-Tri-Tri-no-van-tes!

The Iceni: I-I-I-ce-ni!

Boudicca: They thought they could crush the Iceni!
They thought they could beat Boudicca!
They have beaten my body, but have they broken my spirit?

All: *(Chanting)* No! No! No, no, no!

Boudicca: What has become of their precious Colchester?

All: Dust! Dust! Dust and ashes!

Boudicca: What has become of their precious temple?

All: Dust! Dust! Dust and ashes!

Boudicca: Not quite! Here is the bronze head of their precious Claudius. His bronze body and his bronze horse have been broken into pieces. But this head will sit on a spike in my chariot as I lead you all – to London!

All: To London!

(Exit **the Iceni** *and* **the Trinovantes**.)

SCENE 3

*(**Ursus**, **Tadius**, **Marcus**, **Mannius**, **Varius**, **Didius**, **Lucius** and **Cornelius** march on. They are on their way from Wales to fight Boudicca's army.)*

Soldiers: Eight men in a tent,
Ten tents in a century,
Six centuries in a cohort,
Ten cohorts in a legion!
Our legion is superior –
Up with the Twentieth Valeria!

Ursus: I'm scared. I want my mum.

Tadius: I'm not scared. We put paid to that lot in Wales. Why should we be scared of a rabble in the Midlands?

Marcus: But there are 8,000 of them!

Mannius: And that Boudicca sounds pretty terrifying.

Varius: Did you hear what they did in Colchester?

Didius: No, what?

Varius: Burned the place down and killed everyone!

Lucius: Everyone?

Cornelius: What's up, Lucius? You've gone white.

Lucius: Are you sure they killed everyone?
Even the slaves?

Cornelius: What are you getting at? Oh, I know – that girl you used to fancy all those years ago. What was her name?

Lucius: Jamcilla.

Didius: Come off it, Lucius. Surely your heart's not still in Colchester?

Tadius: It's not just Colchester they've destroyed. They've razed London to the ground, too.

Marcus: And Verulamium.*

Mannius: They're unstoppable.

Lucius: We'll stop them all right. We'll give them such a beating, they'll never get back on their feet!
(Exit the soldiers.)

The river bank in the land of the Iceni. Enter Boudicca, Vilbia and Huctia, looking downcast and weary. Boudicca is carrying the bronze head of Claudius.

Boudicca: This is the place.

Huctia: It's where we came with Father's shield, isn't it, Mother? When we were little?

Vilbia: We were too young to speak to the river goddess then.

Boudicca: But today we can all speak to her.
(She holds out the head)

All: Hear us, goddess of the river.

Boudicca: Our people lie on the battlefield.

Huctia: Our hearts are heavy.

Vilbia: Our lives are ending.

Boudicca: We will soon be drinking, but not of your water.

Huctia: Not of your life.

Vilbia: Our drink will be a drink of death.

Boudicca: We will not be whipped again with Roman whips.

* St. Albans

Huctia: We will not be paraded through the streets of Rome.

Vilbia: We will die here, in the land of the Iceni.

Boudicca: O goddess of the river, take this head.

Huctia: The head of the Emperor who came by water.

Vilbia: The head of the Emperor they worship as a god.

All: Take it into your water.

Boudicca: Send your water to your sisters in the sea.

Huctia: Tell them to carry the Romans back across the water.

Vilbia: Back across the sea to their own land.

*(**Boudicca** lowers the head into the river and they **all** walk away with bowed heads.)*

Sotheby's auction room. It is now 1965, and **Arthur** *and* **Gertie** *are married and in their seventies.* **Arthur** *carries a walking stick.* **Gertie** *puts on a pair of glasses. Enter an* **auctioneer** *with a hammer. She points to the head.*

Auctioneer: Going, going, gone – for £15,500 to the British Museum. *(She brings her hammer down on the table)*

Arthur: £15,500!

Gertie: And you sold it for five shillings!

Arthur: That was over 50 years ago, Gertie.

Gertie: I don't know who I was more angry with – you, or that Mrs. Holland. I bet she knew it was worth more than five bob. And then she had the cheek to tell me I'd never get a maid's job!

Arthur: She had to eat her words when you started working at the vicarage.

SCENE 3

Gertie: Maybe, but I hardly earned anything there, and now her family is getting all this money. Do you realise, Arthur – that £15,500 could be ours? Don't you wish you'd listened to me?

Arthur: No, not really. I've had a good life. The war wasn't much fun, but at least I didn't have to sign up for 25 years like Lucius. And at least I married my slave girl at the end of it!

Gertie: I'm nobody's slave girl!

Arthur: No – on second thoughts, you're more of a Boudicca type.

Gertie: I suppose I've had a better life than Boudicca did. And a longer marriage. Which reminds me – our wedding anniversary's coming up.

Arthur: Nearly half a century!

Gertie: Shall we have a weekend away somewhere to celebrate?

Arthur: Good idea. Where do you fancy? Colchester?

Gertie: Rome, maybe?

*(Enter **Claudius**.)*

Claudius: M-m-may I suggest London? Then you can come and visit me in the B-B-British Museum!

About the play

The play may be either read in class or performed in front of an audience. It will take about 45 minutes.

Staging

There is no need for an elaborate production, and the frequent changes of scene can be suggested with minimal use of props. Most of the props (and actions) can be mimed, e.g. eating, banging in tent pegs, whirling swords, feeding the chickens.

The one really important prop is the bronze head of Claudius, which could be made out of papier mâché. Children might also enjoy making the Eagle of the Twentieth Valeria and the shield which Boudicca sacrifices to the river goddess.

The Godbolds' kitchen table could be constructed from three staging blocks. These could then be separated and arranged as couches for the dining scenes, and then reassembled to form the auctioneer's desk.

The cloth which is wrapped around the head at the beginning of the play could later represent the river. If it is held at each end, Boudicca could sink the shield, and later the head, into its folds.

The pike on which Boudicca carries the head during her rebellion could become Arthur's walking stick when he is an old man. It could also serve as the staff of the Eagle of the Twentieth Valeria.

In Roman time, the play covers the years AD 43, 48, 49 and 60. It is simultaneously set in 1907 and (for the last scene) 1965. You could indicate this with a a scroll for the Roman dates, and a blackboard and chalk for the twentieth-century dates. Two children could be responsible for the chalking and unscrolling, and the scene shifting.

The various battles referred to in the play are scripted to be fought offstage, but you may feel brave enough to stage a mimed battle between the Romans and the Ancient Britons. The sounds of battle can be taped.

Costume

Costumes can also be kept simple. The soldiers could wear baggy T-shirts with belts.

Make togas and stolas (long dresses) from sheets or bedspreads for the Roman nobles.

Boudicca and her daughters could wear long dresses, necklaces and bracelets.

The tribal leaders could have their faces smeared with blue warpaint.

Have fun!

HODDER WAYLAND PLAYS

If you've enjoyed *The Head in the Sand*, try the other titles in the series:

Bombs and Blackberries by Julia Donaldson

Britain is at war, and the Chivers' youngest children have to leave their parents to live in the countryside. They are delighted to be brought back home when it looks as though the Germans aren't going to invade after all. But the air-raid siren goes off and this time it's frighteningly real... This dramatic and touching story is set in Manchester between 1939 and 1941.

Cruel Times by Kaye Umansky

Sissy is doing her best as a kitchen maid to earn the little money on which her Ma and family depend. But when she is robbed by a gang of urchins they face destitution – until she meets Charles Dickens. A tender-hearted story of rich and poor set in Queen Victoria's Britain.

Humble Tom's Big Trip by Kaye Umansky

Humble Tom, a shepherd boy, leaves his country home to see the world. Will he survive the rickety roads, the disgusting diseases, the city crooks and the foul-tasting pottage? This hilarious farce is set in Tudor times around King Henry VIII's voyage to the Field of the Cloth of Gold.

All these books can be purchased from your local bookseller. For more information about Hodder Wayland plays, write to:

The Sales Department, Hodder Children's Books,
A division of Hodder Headline Limited, 338 Euston Road,
London NW1 3BH